Confessions of a Reformed Southern Belle

TOSHA MICHELLE

DEDICATION

I dedicate this to my mother and father. Thank you for instilling in me a
need to create. Your love and support mean the world.

"Oh what a poet I will flay myself into."
— Sylvia Plath

FOREWORD

How do you write a foreword for a book of poetry that has you on the verge of tears, then laughter, then soaring through the high places only a true poet can take you? Hang on, and check your preconceptions, because Tosha Michelle is about to take you on a journey through depths of the heart, and you won't return unchanged.

I have a particular bias in support of this beautiful woman-child, because I am the guy she calls "Dad." I'm actually not her biological father, but I have loved her deeply since before I married her mother when Tosha was eight years old, and I'm pretty sure she feels the same way about me.

She was always a witty little girl, with an incredible imagination and a talent for storytelling. And growing up, she read – a lot. She had some vision difficulties and would hold a book right up to her nose to read, but it seemed like she could read from cover to cover in a few minutes. I'd like to take some credit for her writing, being a writer myself, but I think she soaked it in on her own mostly, through all that reading she did as a child. She developed a love of words and stories and the worlds they transported her to, and her talent blossomed as an adult.

She also spent a lot of time with her grandmother, and around the good folks of the small town of Walhalla, South Carolina, where she absorbed the Southern culture that marked her personality and writing style. She has broken that mold, as the title of this collection hints, but is forever marked by the richness of the Carolina ambiance. The pathos of love lost early in life, recollection of the pains of adolescence and self-doubt still haunt her sometimes, but she has found her salvation through creativity – through expressing those dark feelings in verse, and in her singing. (If you haven't heard that, you're in for another treat.)

I've been a writer and journalist for a long time, and part of that time as an editor. When I read material written by others, I invariably find myself mentally editing, changing things around to the way I would have written them. In this collection, however, I found very little that I would touch as an editor. Tosha has an incomparable sense of rhythm and diction and style that are uniquely hers.

I'm no poetry critic, and I am biased in this case, but I think you'll agree with me that her poetry is for the ages. She'll take you through the depths of melancholy and loneliness with "Yearning," and sing a "Love Song to the South" that will take you back to a simpler, more beautiful time. She'll have you cracking up with a poem about her cat, dancing with her "Goddess of the Night," and ready to take on the world, with "One Voice." One of my favorites is her expression of soaring of the universal soul in the Whitmanesque "Edges."

And everything she writes cries out with the words of the poor little forgotten book on the shelf – Read Me! Go ahead and turn the page.

-- Ron Barnett

Sublime Ends

Remember at the station, waiting
on the train, on that sultry summer day?

We stood, lost in an embrace, breathing in
each other that way -- that awful, terrible,
perfect, mad and delicious way that took us
to the shrouded place.

Remember at the station that day, waiting
on the train, as the wind hummed a lover's tune?

She sang of sublime ends, from supple beginnings --
the alluring medley of serenity in a war of rhyme
on the sharp, bloody edge of Neverland and Narnia,
the peaceful, enchanting interlude of rage & myth.

Remember at the station, that day, as
the train churned closer, and we cussed goodbye?

His steam, a prelude to our eternal kiss, the sun
soaked, never-ending fuel of light, of love, of
heat. Basking and bathing merged and emerged and
submerged, Dancing and swaying in time
with a golden chariot and the huntress.

Remember at the station that day, as
the train tugged away, on an endless track?

We gazed as it came -- as it came -- as it went
Through the crossroads. We did not know,
Our own separate, distant destinations. Our own
rail-less wild paths cut into unimagined mountainsides
You to the west, me to the east.

Remember at the station that day as
the train conducted our last kiss?

That gaping wound where our lips met.
Where we learned cruel fate is hot love and all love is
The calamity of un-armored battle. We all go under.

Wrong or right. Each of our blankets miles and the
ground is nothing but a shifting litter with irascible,
iridescent hope and hurt-dulled dreams, unfulfilled
plans and schemes.

Remember at the station that day, waiting
in the twilight until we forgot and travelled on, and on
 alone, with only prayers of new Twilight to set
in stony slumber with hard solace of old loves lost,
then found again.

Goodbye Neverland

Sunny days, walking along the beach
Collecting fragile seashells and memories;
That must not to be overlooked or forgotten.
Sitting and basking in the sublime breeze
As the tides rolled in, lulling us with a sense of peace.
We talked about books, politics and philosophy
And we argued about the latest trends;
All the while, we reflected on life in all its intricacies,
As we marveled at the crystal blue waters;
Like a marvelous friendship that never seemed to end.
Blanketed by serene winds belonging to no land,
I sat with my lost-boy from Never-Never-land.
The dreamy landscape forever expanding
We were taken away to mystic realms afar.

Suddenly the clouds rolled in,
The wind turned cold and the sky dark and gray.
I reached for your hand, thinking,
We will run and hide from the rain together; but
You were nowhere to be found.
Left alone with the ominous sounds of waves
Crashing on the shore, I called out for you, but
The thunder cracked the air, silencing my breath away.
Where did you go my friend?
I need you now to guide me home.
Who will help me board up the windows?
I cannot secure the house all tight alone all night.
Was it just an illusion, thinking you would stand with me and fight?
How could you leave me alone, battling the storms?
Consumed with pain and fear for our friendship so fragile,
That it could not withstand mere earthly elements.
Just like a storm, we grew together, raining our tears,
Until we ceased to be; just as a storm ends, bringing about
The inevitable clear blue skies of fair weather, friend.

Yearning

Nostalgia enters.
Melancholy takes her cue.
Tantalizing and haunting melodies fill the air.
Sitting transfixed, lost in echoes of the past --
Nostalgia is lost in a reminiscent trance.
Clinging to ephemeral dreams
Melancholy's carnival of variegated colors
Illuminates the stage in her mind
Whilst churning away through the scenery of her mind.
Memories linger...
Revelations of the soul's misdirection
Unveil a plot left untold.
Remorse...regrets...the awful longing that always comes-
With bittersweet remembrances of
Myths of love promised forever.
The mist-bound dreamer chained to chords of reasons
Recalls an ancient season.
The lights go up, the curtain falls
Leaving the audience to wonder and
Longing for another chance to
Make Love to one true romance.

Wasteland

Apathy, your momentous
Tune lulls us to sleep.
In our somber slumber
Dreaming dreamless dreams.

Solace is found in the mind-
Numbing hypnotic sound.
In our cationic state,
There is no hope, no pain.
Only blissful unawareness.

In our hibernation
We are safe from-
Addiction,
War,
Famine,
Genocide,
Poverty,
Racism.
They don't exist
In our drowsy bliss.

Silent and unaware
We doze on as the world
Spins Madly on
Raging on
Warring on.

We lay lost;
Entranced in the
Sublime banality of
A shadow of leafless,
Fruitless trees.

Read Me

In a lovely little book store, in a beautiful little town
There lived a freshly printed book named, Read Me.
She was leather-bound with crisp, clean, bright pages
Full of depth and secrets to be revealed, with a beautiful story to tell.
The little book was filled with joy and promise.
If one listens close enough, you could hear her happy cries of---

Read Me!

Days went by, and people would come in and admire her odd but
unique cover.
Some would even pick her up and run their hands along her spine and
remark, what a lovely little book.
Invariably though, they would be distracted by another book that caught
their eye
Or be in a rush to be on their way,
As life was hectic and demanding, and there was no time to delay.
Still the little book would cry as they walked out the door.
Come back...don't you want to---

Read Me!

The seasons went by, and still the people would pass through
Always noting the strange little book. Some would even open the cover
And flip through her pages, but no one ever delved too deeply. If they
had, they would have
Noted all the words that filled up the pages with humor and despair,
with love and disdain; it was
A simple, yet complex tale, a story just waiting to be told.
And every day the book still cried with hope and faith---

Read Me!

Years were gone now, and so were the people.
The town had a new book store that offered coffee, and the latest best
sellers.
By now the little book was frayed around the edges, her binding cracked
from years of handling,
Her pages faded and yellow.
"Oh, who will read me now," she thought, "I am broken."
The little book had all but given up hope.

She felt like a prisoner high on the shelf.
Now she only half-heartedly whispered---

Read me.

One cold evening as the little book sat despondent and alone,
She was startled to hear the door of the store open.
By this time though, she dared not hope that anyone would read her;
still, she could not help but be drawn
To the man standing across the room -- where did he come from?
Was he looking at her? As he moved closer, the little book had no
expectation that he would pick her up.
Surely he was like the rest and would only pass her by or peruse her
cover, remark on her
Quirkiness and be on his way.
Suddenly, and to her complete and utter surprise, he pulled her down
from the shelf.
Oh no, surely after all this time, could it be someone was finally going
to---

Read Me!

Like all the others, he ran his hands along her cover.
Here we go again, thought the little book, but there was something
different about this man.
He touched her with reverence and tenderness.
It felt like he already knew her story, but how could that be?
No one had ever bothered to learn her cover to cover.
Odder still, she felt she knew this man and had known him since her
conception.
The man spoke softly and said, "little book; I am your reader, and I am
here to set you free.
I know a secret, and I want you to share your secrets with me."
Right then and there the little worn book started to feel new again, even
though her pages were still
Frayed and her binding still a mess, somehow it did not matter now that
he had arrived.
She knew at last this man, her reader, would be the one, finally to---
Read Me!

See Me

Do you know me?
The girl behind the glasses
The girl in the dress
The one who has spent her life
Lost in books and quiet meditation.
Sheltered from the world of hurt.
But still always questioning her worth.
The girl who had lived her life
Behind guarded humor
And a world of dreams
Hiding.
Afraid of ridicule
Harsh critique
Shallow judgments
And illicit schemes
A friend of caution.
Always existing just to please.
Focusing on everyone's else's need.
Do you know me?
The girl behind the glasses
What lies beneath the surface
Of that woman child called, ME.

Riddle Me This

Dancing with time…in time…to an open mind.
Seeking to find an answer to this infinite rhyme.
Befuddled, emerged, in waves of the mystic and sublime.
This maze that is my head. Riddled thoughts.
Existentialism in a metaphoric Labyrinth.
Striving to be authentic in character and spirit.
In a world that is nothing but absurd and banal.
Tick, tock chimes the clock.
Do I dare to understand?
To seek and find
The answers that lie
In an addled head.
Infinity squared.

Freedom

Set your spirit free
Find peace in the rain pouring down.
Look for the path where trust is a friend.
Blanket the earth with words of love.
Compassion and tolerance.
Negativity will not win.
Bask in hope.
Faith is the catalyst
The inner light from within.

Goddess of The Night

A shy smile, a heartfelt glance.
High heels, dancing in the moonlight.
Starlit dreams.
Sparkling with love and happiness.
She feels like a goddess.
Queen of the night.
Laughing like an angel.
Living on a dare.
A soul set free.
Channeling the beautiful thing.

Awakened

A chaotic mind and restless heart
Find themselves submerged and
Emerging, from an orderly
Tranquilized sea of life;
Riding waves of despair and hope
While the winds of time and change
Fueled by the fires of change and time
Make a dance of chance
With an unknown, yet
Well known tune.

I can't explain the yearning in my heart
The music that consumes my soul
Secrets I keep from you
 Dissonant chords clashing

Her restive heart and chagrined mind
Is swooning to his knowing tune, which
Lifts her away into night's bright skies
Feeling and knowing sunlight's sway;
She feels and knows her enchantment is
But one chance dance away,
Awaiting, for their mythical dreams'
Marvelous reified awakening.

City Haze

Dance with me in the city haze,
Through September grooves,
under the beauty of the harvest moon,
in patterned fields of amber.
Colored by a heavenly mist, dust of serenity.
We'll set the night ablaze.
While the shadows enfold us
as the willow whispers
And the wind sings us a melodic tune.
Our imagination sets the beat.
We'll find solace and cohesion,
As the melancholy drains away
on cracked sidewalks of urban decay

Shades of Gray

Melancholy is one of my dearest friends.
She arrives on gray clouds at dusk
Riding on the winds of nostalgia.
Bringing her dark mood, she hovers
Shrouded in a veil of somber solitude.
She lingers, taunting the senses with what could have been.
Consumed by the shadows, sorrow prevails.

Diversity of Differences

To deny equality to one is to deny equality for all.
We won't find joy by misplacing our unhappiness onto others.
Love cannot be defined, assigned or mitigated.
 It's not something to be controlled or dictated.
Love is uncontrollable and limitless.

To deny one's life, is to play God.
Who are we to decide who lives or dies?
Life ends for all of us.
Maybe we should be more concerned about living our own lives
And not depriving others of their right to live freely.

It time we grew up and came to grasp just how vast our world is.
It's much greater than the human race, yet we are shocked when it
retaliates.
It's not just about you and me.
We need to step outside our cultural sandboxes and learn to live with
one another.
It's not just about our beliefs and community.
There are multitudes of diversity, beyond the playground of our minds.
Look beyond the stereotypes, discrimination,
And bigotry. Those things have no place here.

The possibilities for humankind are endless, but we'll never realize,
The potential until we understand and embrace the uniqueness that is
the world.

My Lost Love

Sleep, remember when we couldn't get enough of each other?
When we were in perfect sync?
You were my sweet oblivion, my haven,
And all I wanted at the end of a long day.
I couldn't get my fill of you.
You consumed my thoughts,
My body constantly longing for the sweet release,
I always found in you.
We'd come together every night in blissful harmony.
I'd lose myself in your sweet repose.
Do you recall the days of satin and lavender, of dreams and peaceful slumber?
I do, and I miss you

Nothing

Narcissism is the new black;
Self-absorption, the latest trend,
Shallow and superficial.
Walk down a runway of banality.
While it's "All About Me" plays in the background.
Accessorized by a callous disregard.
Dressed up in a pretty package.
With nothing underneath.
Hollow and empty
A model of vapidness.
The latest in fashion is only skin deep.
Maybe…one-day…unselfishness and humility will be in vogue again.
Until then, did you see the latest picture of me?

Lyre

Words in a book,
Call to me like the daughters of the river god
Getting lost between the pages.
I hide between the lines.
Finding comfort
Cover to cover.
Submerging myself in prose
Drowning in poetic metaphors.
An Odyssey of an open mind.

Wrecked Head

Some days I am lucid and full of wisdom
But then there are those days when my mind
Is invaded by hoarders, the clutter
Littering my brain.
In these times, I am lost as to where to begin.
There's no filtering my thoughts.
My mind is in overdrive.
Like a hyperactive teen strung out on meth,
My eyes glazed over, lost in a surreal dream.
A million thoughts float around me.
I try to grasp just one.
But they are elusive,
Just beyond my reach.
All I can do is wait.
For gravity and clarity to kick back in

Lost

Lost in an endless wasteland of insipidness.
Not knowing who to trust.
Groping around in the darkness.
Seeking light and renewal.
Lost with no direction.
With no compass to guide me.
Lost in my thoughts,
A labyrinth of confusion
Lost in the past, with an uncertain future.
What will be my path?
Lost in worry, endless drifting.
With so many decisions still left to be made.
Lost, yet not forgotten
Hope's flame still burns.
Knowing somehow, someday, the tables will turn.

Feel the Chemical Kicking In

Sadness creeps up my spine,
Sneaking up, covering my eyes.
Taking my breath.
Stealing my serenity.
Melancholy rains down.
I try to shake it off.
The drops linger.
Peace, just beyond my reach.
Floating out in space without me.

Edges

I am a child throwing rocks into the stream.
Challenging the rushing water.
Raising my fist and daring fate to do it worst.
I am a dancer in the waves of the ocean.
Swaying in time with the tide.
Pirouetting, the current my only friend.
I am the sun, rising across the canyon
Ascending, and shinning down.
Giving the illusion of perception and motion.
I am thoughts like a rolling river.
Water cascading over the rocks of my soul.
Shaping, forming, conforming.
I am the peace of the rain forest.
Basking in solitude
Tranquil, serene, transfixing angles.
Reflecting from within.
Dripping and dropping. Shaking it off.
I am the dust of the galaxy.
Yearning to know itself.
I am the wind.
Wandering. Searching.
A storm brewing from within.

Things to do at 4 a.m.

Get drunk on words
Drown in their essence
Submerge in the constellations
That plague my mind.
Dizzy from the broken
Tattered memories
That invade my space.
I write.

Spring Cleaning

Removing all of the clutter and debris
that litters my thoughts and mind.
Dusting the past away.
Ordering chaos,
Seeing what's hidden,
under the sofa cushions of
My poor addled brain.
Intuition, my broom
Sweeping away the vestiges of
my self's doubt.
Vacuuming up insecurities,
scrubbing away the cynicism as
As I polish up long-held dreams.
Spring cleaning with
Pen and paper as
my only needed tools.

One Voice

I am one voice, just one voice, but
Strong and proud is my voice.
I am one person, just one person
Who strives to stand out from the crowd.
Sometimes I find myself surrendering to
The naysayers surrounding me, who talk so loud
They drown out my voice with their droning sounds.
I cannot sit silently and expect my stillness
To provoke any changes, for
That is to be devoid of reason
Giving others season for no reason;
I must squash the fear
Stand on my own two feet
And testify to the love I feel and
Be a voice that resonates and
Resounds across the universe
Arousing in others in due season
The flames of their own
Impassioned reasons…
To keep on striving in not only the battle
But the journey, the road less traveled,
Littered with rocky terrain and
Fraught with perils around every bend;
Love and hope must lead the way,
Beseeching us onward
Towards infinite harmony,
Beyond the limits of humanity's mortal minds
To change the world, to make an impact
That goes beyond the core
Into the depths of chaos and despair,
To redefine peace from something temporal,
Into that, which is permanent and
Forever affirming life, giving birth to love
Forever and ever, beyond time's last day.
Like the sun that rises and sets
Leaving its mark even after it goes down;
Signifying hope and renewal,
Illuminating the darkness,
Burning bright, hot and strong.
Bringing growth and life with
The birth of a new dawn --

I too want to change the world.

Love Song to the South

Magnolias in bloom
Honeysuckles on the vine.
Basking in the lazy rays.
Of sweet sunshine.
Summers down by the lake.
Drinking strawberry wine.
Night falls
Singing the tune of a Carolina moon.
Dancing in time with fireflies.
Living beam, sparking light.
On a sultry evening that feels so right.
She calls to me.
Riding in an old Ford truck.
Papa at the wheel.
Little girl beside him.
His Junebug filled with love.
Granny with her Irish eyes
Sits on her other side.
Off on a grand adventure.
Either down by the sandy coast.
Or high up in the Smokies.
Either way, it does not matter.
Sure to see the beautiful things.
Simple and lovely.
Palmettos trees, seagulls flapping, waves crashing.
Tall majestic peaks, vistas of blue and green.
These are the moments to keep.
She calls to me.
Lying on a blanket.
Staring at the clouds.
Daffodils swaying in the breeze
Bumblebees buzz around,
Braves game on the radio
Cheering with the crowd.
Sunday go to meeting.
Singing In the Sweet Bye and Bye
Granny cut a hickory if you get out of line.
Dinner on the table.
Chicken fried.
Collard greens and maters.
Dessert? Well. Maybe later.

She calls to me.
A chill in the air
Leaves falling to the ground
College football becomes the reason.
Carolina or Clemson
Who will win this season?
Sitting on the porch swing.
Guitar making a country sound.
Feet tapping, Hands clapping.
Drinking sweet tea
Life in a Southern town.
She calls to me.
Mistletoe and holly
Aunts and uncles surround.
Grandpa is feeling jolly.
Gifts are passed around.
Heads bowed; hands clasped.
Amazing Grace, how sweet the sound.
Pass the turkey and gravy
Peace and love abound.
That soulful, spiritual tune.
One of old mixed with the new.
Kinship and friendship.
Love and war;
Heartache and hate.
Renewal and Survival
A bittersweet revival.
A prayer, a curse,
Sweet rhyme and verse.
She calls to me.

Stay

Stay with me
And sit awhile
On the porch
In the swing
And sway
With me.
Stay with me
Hold my hand
Sing to me
Tell me stories
Of magic and pixie dust,
Of wrestling with dragons,
Riding unicorns,
Of a valiant prince, and
The damsel he so loved
Of Narnia and Elysium,
Far beyond, the looking glass
Before the Pied Piper plays his tune,
Before the clock strikes midnight,
Before the wolf bares his teeth,
Before the hourglass runs out,
While there's still time,
To wish upon a star,
Stay with me
And sit awhile
On the porch
In the swing
And sway
While once upon a time
Slowly fades away…

Mr. Elite

Mr. Elite, with a rose in his lapel,
Wearing a condescending smile,
A mask of civility and refinement,
Underneath he is repelled.
A girl in a vintage dress, demure and shy,
Humble visage, wanting only to impress.
A heartfelt smile, a beguiling sigh.
She briefly catches his eye.
Her apprehended affections,
Cast aside like bad tasting wine.
Mr. Elite, with the rose in his lapel,
Slowly watched as the flower fell.
And upon descending left a black spot
a permanent mark.
The proud flower,
in all its bold and illustrious wonder.
The sheen of propriety. Gone.
Tarnish by a callous disregard.
Mr. Elite for a second wavered in his shallow ways.
But for the girl, the rose had lost its luster.

My Emotion

If I were to write a poem,
It would be about you.
I'd paint you with phrases,
In vibrant shades of many hues
Portraying your image, as
Evocative and coaxing,
Portraying you, as
The provocateur of
My heart's one and only muse.

If I were to write a poem,
You would be my ballad.
Free verse my means of articulation.
No rhyme or meter, but
Pure verse of which
None is sweeter.

If I were to write a poem,
It would be an ode to you.
No hyperbole or extended metaphors.
Devoid of contradictions and connotations,
Just simple plain words of
Love and truth, as
The one and only one
For whom this one is meant to be.

If I were to write a poem,
You would be my inspiration.
I would be a vessel.
Words once lost, now found.
Whimsical, elemental, eternal
Become my poetry of
You in motion, as
My one
Emotion…

Letting Go

Autumn leaves falling off tall, stately trees.
Dancing embers in transition, falling
Creating dust like gold full of somber wonders.
The tree has learned the art of letting go.
It is not afraid to stand alone, its branches bare.
It knows and accepts life's rhythm;
Birds are leaving their nest,
Flying away into abstract blue,
Singing their haunting freedom song, like
Psalms of divine inspiration,
They too know the art of letting go.
The tide effortlessly rolling out to sea,
As it caresses the shore one last time, with its
Crashing waves kissing the sand
Leaving only its foam and
A majestic roar in its wake, as
Nature takes her course,
Mother Earth teaches us the art of letting go

Skin-Soaked Madness

I know it may sound cliché.
But kiss me in the pouring rain.
Draw me near, my dear.
Whisper my name.
As a divine revelation
Push me up against the wall
Hands in my hair.
Lips and bodies entwined.
As our hearts beat faster.
The pheromones between us
Stealing our air.
Fervent kisses in the rain.
Connecting the place where
Desire and hope meet.
Sending a message from fingertips
To toes, and straight into our souls.
Droplets are falling faster.
As we become enraptured.
Stardust-kissed illuminations.
Spirits soaring wild and free.
Getting drenched in skin-soaked madness.
Basking in the cloud's teardrops.
Tenderness and passion raining down

Kicking Pollyanna to the Curb.

Removing my rose colored glasses.
Stepping down from my Ivory Tower.
Into a broken world.
Kicking Pollyanna to the curb.
Yesterday everything was disposable.
Self-pity was my guide.
Always crying wolf.
For the suffering I had known.
Today the bubble burst.
Choking on my own callous disregard.
Slapping me out of my apathetic slumber.
To hell with selfishness and pride.
Eyes wide open. The blinders off
My heart cries...my soul aches
For the child who's never known love.
Only abuse and neglect.
For the man in need of a home.
Making a bed out of concrete and stone.
For the drug addict who's fallen through the cracks.
Who can't find her way back.
For empty bellies and a cruel world.
The sex slave being pimped on the street.
Only 15 years old, her body bought and sold.
For war-torn countries, surrounded by senseless death.
Genocide, mutilated figures, horrific acts...all in the name of hate.
Smashing my rose colored glasses against the wall of apathy.
Tearing down the Ivory Tower.
I live in the light of grace.
Vowing to be a voice for change.
To take a stand, to never lie down in complacency again.
My shield, hope. My sword, compassion.
Eyes wide open in clarity and love.

Ring the bell

The voice in my head.
A death knell
Wreaking havoc on my soul.
An Epitaph of
You're not pretty enough.
You're not smart enough.
You'll never be good enough.
The tolling of the bell.
Killing my self-confidence.
Laying to rest my dreams.

Can that which is dead be resurrected?
Can I rediscover the beauty that's always been?
To be twice born.
The power within,
Silence, the voice in my head

For whom the bell tolls.
Not for me, not this time.
I'll ring my own bell.
One of liberty and laureate
Church bells on a Sunday morning.
Life renewing, lyrical cheerful ... clanging hope.
Rebirth and revival ... renewal and survival.
There's beauty in imperfections.
My mind is strong. I am enough.
Letting go of self-doubt.
Reclaiming my dreams.
A mind made anew.

Lost and Found

Searching for the path to peace,
the soft glow of solace,
a warm embrace,
a haven from heartache and pain.
Longing to dwell in faith and love
Life-affirming hope coursing
through my veins.
Darkness can only eclipse the sun for so long.
I know there will come a day,
when my thoughts are as clear
as a morning sunrise.
Happy as a child's laughter
I'll find the path to serenity and revival.
Where struggles fade and the world
is full of promise again.
I'll no longer mourn the past.
or get lost in what could have been.
I'll find the road to renewal and survival
Carried on the wings of a prayer.

A Mother's Love

Her presence gives me courage.
Her light guides my way.
She fashions my dreams
And paints my hope.
She give love without conditions.
Forgiveness without reservations.
Accepts me as I am.
Judgment has no place
A mother's love is the
Greatest love.
It knows no barriers or bounds.
Distance and time can't mar its grace
A love as constant as the waves and the sand.
Elemental, eternal, everlasting.

Ode to Tucker

My cat can rock. My cat can roll.
He knows how to keep with the beat,
Dancing around in the street.
My cat can recite Shakespeare with ease
You see, he's fluent in CATonese
My cat is king of all he surveys.
Mostly, he surveys his food bowl.
My cat is an expert at snoozing.
Who knows, perhaps, he's been boozing.
My cat is the greatest of muses.
Poets and writers he inspires.
My cat is cool...the coolest of the cool.
He'll snort his nip. And not give a...ahem
My cat is a saint and a sinner.
His whole world revolves around dinner.
My cat is a superior
Just look at his posterior.
My cat is the greatest.
And now it's been stated.
My cat will never be overrated.

A Upon a Time Once

What once was,
but never was.
A story left untold.
Tomorrow's forever forestalled.
Today's regrets,
Yesterday's dreams.
Memories turned cold.
Lost in bittersweet's
What could have been.

Real Love

Once upon a time in a land called Life, there lived a thing called Real Love. Now, while it's true, that Real Love is often the stuff fairy tales are made of, it can only last so long running off fairy dust. Real love, the lasting kind, is always firmly rooted in reality. You see, even the Prince and Princess would argue over crowns being left on the floor and how to run the kingdom. They understood that to live happily ever after, they had to accept that Real Love is not just butterflies in the tummy...sometimes, it feels more like heartburn. Through the years they came to the realization that Real Love is made up of things like commitment, compromise, consistency, loyalty, riding the highs and the lows, and hard work. It's about trust and allowing each other to grow and BE. It creates its own kind of magic and tenacity. Real Love is sacred, profane, mundane, extraordinary, heaven and hell -- and the only love worth fighting for.

I wrote the poem below for my mentor and dear friend Colin Smith. He had just turned fifty the time.

CAPTAIN SCARLET
I

"Every since I was a child all my dreams been running wild"

A baby is born with the heart of a warrior.
A restless spirit, a soul full of magic
In need of a place to call his own.
Into his life walks a beautiful woman.
Singing to him her sweet motherly song.
He will be her son now, and she will be his protection and hope.
These are the days of security and peace.
A blessed refuge and reprieve, but alas not meant to be.

II
"Hate is like a battle, love is like a war"

A little boy grows feeling lost and alone.
Clinging to his mother, she alone is his home.
Escaping from his father who is militant and mean,
Berated and bullied it's always a scene.
He loses himself in rockets and dreams.
These are the days of fear and survival,
Where contempt and abuse are his arch rivals.

III
"My adolescent dreams are nightmares in the streams."

A teenager he becomes, defiance his mantra,
He's out on the streets, looking for peace.
Drugs and needles he seeks. Hedonism and Dionysus he meets.
A life on the brink Chaos and havoc he reaps.

These are the days of excess and rebellion
A manic season of an outlaw and hellion.

IV
"We're the kids from the block we know how to rock."

Adulthood finds him a punk rocker with the band.
Girls and guitars, he's pissing on czars.
His future looks grand. A rebel is taking a stand.
JJ, The Cardinal, -The Blood is the plan.
These are the days of desires and extremes,
Fighting the establishment and rocking sweet, sultry things.

V
"Loving you religiously is doing in my brain."

A man full grown now at 25 he's half-way to today.
The girl of his dreams, a bonnie lass is she,
He takes as his bride and a life of passion they lead.
In a few years, a daughter comes along.
Filling her daddy's heart with song
These are the days of stability and chaos,
Anguish and bliss, and love not without risks.

VI
" I don't want fortune. I don't want fame. I want a piece of history."

A time of changes comes on strong with 30's drumbeat marching on.
His mind begins yearning as he develops a hunger for learning,
His thoughts, they are a turning, his soul burning.
Off to college, he goes. The seeds of knowledge sown.
These are the days of highs and lows,
Of books and enlightenment and he grows.

VII
"The bouquet of insanity left me a wreck, but I won't forget."

The 40"s find him on his own; his family gone.
Somehow, somewhere, someway it all went wrong,
Some things in life are not meant to be.
Sorrow is all he sees, but time moves on.
Through adversity, he finds his strength.
The depth of his spirit, humanity is his link.
Finding his Magna Charta, he realized his purpose.
Justice and liberty become his new song,
A magnum opus for us all.
These are the days of devotion and emotions,
His soul for humanity is causing a commotion.

VIII
"The road less traveled, it's the one I'm own"

At 50 now what will be will be.
He has miles to go before he sleeps; He cannot rest life is still a
test,
But his future is anything but bleak, His spirit far from weak.
Riding out the highs and lows, Tempering the desires and
extremes,
Ordering security and chaos, Challenging the unchallengeable
dream.
Understanding from experience, he fights the true outlaws and
hellions
Humanity his devotion.. Lost in emotions

These will be the days of Renewal and Survival. Rebirth and
Revival
A rebel causing a commotion, a life in full motion

Sweet Tea Musings

In every life, there's always a moment
Where we lose ourselves
And the gray takes over.
Colorized in shades of black and blue
there are times
Where all we see is a haze of yellow
and we find ourselves
Basking in the warmth of assurance.
A mirage of transcendental tones,
Self and not self
Doership and discipleship
we wrestle with reality and myth.
Creating distinctions in the labyrinth of our minds,
Painting on a canvas
Of the ridiculous and sublime
Ruminating upon
Thoughts of power,
Fate and choice
Salted, peppered, and sprinkled,
With philosophical introspection,
of purple, green and dazzling shades of
The Existential who?
The seas, the sky,
Me, myself
And I,

Creating, defining,
Defying, perplexing,
Pondering, wondering,
Wandering oxygen becomes fire
With red being the only hue.

Not Just a Girl

Inside she is sunshine.
An innocent girl.
Full of dreams.
Her whole life ahead of her.
The world at her feet.
Out on the street
In the late summer heat.
Men with wicked schemes.
She meets
They have her in their reach.
Sadness and horror they teach.
Selling her to the highest bidder.
Money they will keep.
Binding her in chains.
A sex slave they seek.
Breaking her spirit.
Crushing her soul.
Taking her humanity.
All for gold.
Inside she is broken.
A heart that just a shell.
Her body void and empty.
Her life a living hell.
The terror gets worse.
Fear it grows.
Brutality all she knows
Can anyone hear her?

She is only 12 years old

Join in the fight against Modern Day Slavery. You can make a difference. If you believe you have information about a potential trafficking situation:

Call the National Human Trafficking Resource Center (NHTRC) toll-free hotline at 1-888-373-7888:
http://www.traffickingresourcecenter.org/report-trafficking

ACKNOWLEDGMENTS

There are so many people to thank. Please forgive me if I leave anyone out. I must start by expressing my undying love and gratitude to my family. Randy, Tiffany, Taylor and even a rock star cat, Tucker, you guys are the best kind of crazy. I love you. Thank you for the support and inspiration. To my dad, Ron Barnett, you embody love and gentleness. In addition, you are a stellar editor. Your instinct and insight were invaluable in the creation of this book. To my mom, you will always be my hero and the coolest person I know. To Lois Murphy Hawkins, my grandmother, I miss you every day.

Jane Rothman, my fellow Chit Chat Chicks and snark wielding ninja. Thanks for the love and friendship. James Dennard, you'll always be Niles to my Frasier. Heather Culford, you are my role model in all things pest. Bruno Gunn, we're looking at you. Randy Hampton, you're still like the brother I wish I never had. Kidding. Nothing but love. To the pool boy gang and what a gang it is: Jennifer Berry-Bross, Diane Grechoski, Donna Tibbett Stevens, Larry White, Ian Lim, Sandy Milos, Ron Haney, Laura Roth Patton, Trish Robertson Ferch, Amy Hillgren Peterson, Lisa Wilson Piwonka, Michael G., Terry DeMeo, Todd Lowe, Lesa Grant Feazel, Skip Treaster, Keith Rey, Andy Behrman (Electroboy), Tammy Darnell. Sabine Flynn. I adore you all. When's our next adventure?

I'd be remiss if I left out SR's angels. Brown Angel Eyes, Renata, Kez, Alexandra, Lady C, Lady, J, Chris Emerson Grey, Raven_Argyle_Sister and the lovely Ellen Totten. You ladies are a force of nature. Thanks for the kindness; it truly is never wasted.

Finally, to anyone who happens upon this book. Thank you for taking a chance on it and me. I've always loved poetry, even from a young age; there's something magical that comes from the reading and recitation of a lyrical poem. My poetry is deeply personal and a reflection of myself, flaws and all. I certainly do not claim to be a poet laureate. I'm still very much a neophyte I simply write to know myself better. It's a way to make the unknown, known, the unseen, visible, to make the intangible, tangible. I don't have to temper or water down my emotions when I write. I can give voice to my insecurities, my passions and my inner melancholy beast.

Writing for me is cathartic and healing. I believe art should be a force for good. It is my hope that, my humble verses will strike a chord with humanity that something in my words with resonant, that you will find a little of yourself in my musings.

ABOUT THE AUTHOR

A reformed Southern Belle, who lives to write, thrives on creativity, earning degrees and majoring in snark. A lifelong devotee of Godiva chocolates, so hide your sweets. A human rights advocate and lover of all things feline and girly.

Learn more at www.laliterati.com

Twitter @taraleigh2020